Abersoch

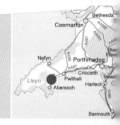

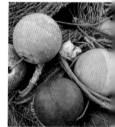

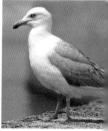

Well marked coast path, beaches and a quiet lane through a caravan park

Wales Coast Path
Llŷn Peninsula

Text: *Carl Rogers and Sioned Bannister*

Photographs: *Carl Rogers, Tony Bowerman, mikeatkinson.net, Visit Wales, Shutterstock*

Design: *Carl Rogers*

Northern Eye Books
ISBN 978-1-908632-12-8

A CIP catalogue record for this book is available from the British Library

www.northerneyebooks.co.uk

Important Advice: The routes described in this book are undertaken at the reader's own risk. Walkers should take into account their level of fitness, wear suitable footwear and clothing, and carry food and water. It is also advisable to take the relevant OS map with you in case you get lost and leave the area covered by our maps.

Whilst every care has been taken to ensure the accuracy of the route directions, the publishers cannot accept responsibility for errors or omissions, or for changes in the details given. Nor can the publisher and copyright owners accept responsibility for any consequences arising from the use of this book.

If you find any inaccuracies in either the text or maps, please write or email us at the address below. Thank you.

First published in 2012 by
Northern Eye Books Limited
Northern Eye Books, Tattenhall, Cheshire CH3 9PX
Email: tony@northerneyebooks.com
For sales enquiries, please call 01928 723 744

Cover: *Mynydd Mawr and Bardsey*

Contents

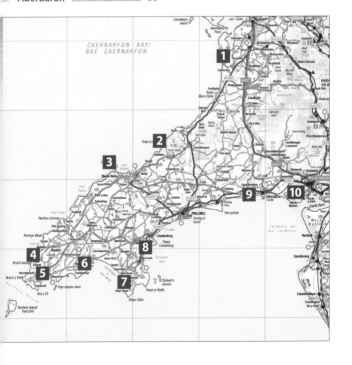

The **Wales Coast Path**

WALES IS THE ONLY COUNTRY IN THE WORLD with a path around its entire coast. The long-distance **Wales Coast Path** offers 870 miles/1400 kilometres of unbroken coastal walking, from the outskirts of the walled city of Chester in the north to the market town of Chepstow in the south.

There's something new around every corner. Visually stunning and rich in both history and wildlife, the path promises ever-changing views, wildflowers and seabirds, as well as castles, coves and coastal pubs. In fact, the Wales Coast Path runs through 1 Marine Nature Reserve, 2 National Parks, 3 Areas of Outstanding Natural Beauty, 11 National Nature Reserves, 14 Heritage Coasts, and 23 Historic Landscapes. And, to cap it all, the **Wales Coast Path** links up with the long-distance Offa's Dyke Path at either end: creating a complete, 1,030 mile circuit of the whole of Wales.

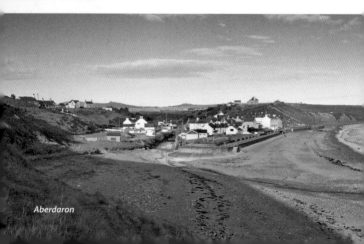

Aberdaron

The **Llŷn Peninsula**

The Llŷn peninsula pushes 30 miles into the Irish Sea, tipped by the holy isle of Bardsey, or Ynys Enlli—'the island of 20,000 saints'. This remote landscape is characterised by traditional farms and compact villages, punctuated by volcanic hills. Its relative isolation has made it a haven for the Welsh language and culture.

Sea cliffs, offshore rocks and intimate coves dominate the northern coast, while the gentler southern coast promises sandy beaches and holiday towns like Abersoch and Pwllheli. But for sheer beauty, tranquillity and wildlife, Llŷn is hard to beat.

"I have crawled out at last, far as I dare on to a bough, of country that is suspended, between sky and sea. From what was I escaping?"

Collected Poems, R S Thomas, vicar of Aberdaron

TOP 10 **Walks:** Llŷn Peninsula

THE LLŶN PENINSULA offers some of the finest coastal walking in North Wales. In just over 80 miles there are dramatic sea cliffs, quiet coves, wide sandy bays, two medieval castles, tiny fishing villages, a pub on the beach, a number of coastal hills and a hidden valley. The walks in this book are what we consider to be the finest routes along this superb section of coast, one of the eight main sections of the **Wales Coast Path**.

Dinas Dinlle — page 8

Nant Gwrtheyrn — page 14

Porth Dinllaen — page 18

Whistling Sands — page 24

Yr Eifl (The Rivals) from Dinas Dinlle

Dinas Dinlle

An easy amble that explores an Iron Age hillfort, a spectacular beach and a nature reserve

What to expect:
Good footpaths and quiet lanes. Some paths can be muddy after rain. One ascent to hillfort

Distance/time: 7km / 4.5 miles. Allow 2 hours

Start: Seafront car park in Dinas Dinlle (beside toilets and café)

Grid ref: SH 436 567

Ordnance Survey Map: Explorer 254 *Lleyn Peninsula East: Porthmadog, Criccieth & Pwllheli*

After the walk: Beach cafés in Dinas Dinlle (summer months only) or plenty of cafés, pubs and restaurants in Caernarfon

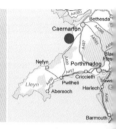

Walk outline

A short ascent leads to the top of the Dinas Dinlle Iron Age hillfort with its stunning views on a clear day. The walk then leads north along the edge of the shore, before heading inland towards the vast tidal inlet of Foryd Bay, a nature reserve that teems with wildlife and birds. The return journey is made along a quiet lane and through pretty farmland before returning to the shore.

Dinas Dinlle

Dinas Dinlle is the site of an Iron Age hillfort, almost half of whose once impressive ramparts have now been eroded by the sea. The stunning views from the summit, however, remain: making it well worth the short climb. On a clear day you can see southwest along the coast towards Yr Eifl, on Llŷn; north towards Holyhead Mountain on Anglesey; and south and east to the mountains of Snowdonia.

Aviation museum

The nearby tidal inlet of Foryd Bay is a haven for wildlife and a designated Nature Reserve. The sand, mud flats and saltmarsh attract huge numbers of migrating and native birds. Waders and wildfowl seen here include oystercatchers, curlews, lapwings, greenshanks and terns.

Curlew

The Walk

1. Face the sea and turn left towards the prominent glacial hillock of **Dinas Dinlle**, passing the café. Bear left through the gate to follow the path to the top of the hill.

Explore the eroded ramparts and enjoy the panoramic views, then retrace your steps back to the seafront. Pass the car park on the right and continue along the tarmac path that runs along the top of the beach.

Follow this elevated path for 1 mile / 1.5 kilometres or so, with **Caernarfon Bay** spanning the horizon out to the left and the reclaimed marshland of **Morfa Dinlle** on your right. Continue on the tarmac path until it reaches a small parking area close to the airport perimeter fence.

2. Turn right here to follow the lane ahead, passing the speed restriction signs and then the **Aviation Museum** and the entrance to **Caernarfon Airport**.

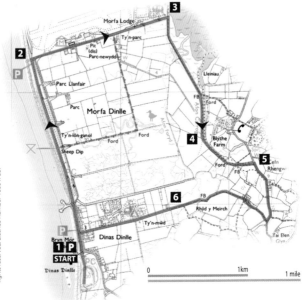

Tidal estuary: *The vast tidal estuary of Foryd Bay with the distant outlines of Bwlch Mawr and Yr Eifl (The Rivals)*

During the Second World War Caernarfon Airport was used as an RAF base, but it is now a small airfield used mainly for flying lessons and pleasure flights over the Llŷn Peninsula. There is also an interesting aviation museum that is open from March to October.

Ignore a right turning and continue ahead to pass the entrance to **Morfa Lodge Holiday Park**, beyond which the road turns into a rough track.

3. At the end of the track, go through the kissing gate and turn right along the top of the broad, earthen embankment of the sea defences that protect the western flank of **Foryd Bay**.

Foryd Bay was once part of a vast saltmarsh called Morfa Dinlle that covered all the land that is now the airfield and holiday park. But following the nineteenth-century 'Enclosing and Embanking of Lands Act', much of the marsh was reclaimed for farmland.

Today, Foryd Bay's 700 acres of saltmarsh and mudflats are a Local Nature Reserve that's home to a wide variety of wildfowl

Glorious views: *The elevated summit of Dinas Dinlle gives superb views across Caernarfon Bay to Yr Eifl in clear weather*

and waders. Look out for grey herons, redshanks, curlews, turnstones and little ringed plovers.

Follow the embankment-top path until you reach a small footbridge. Ignore this and keep on along the embankment as it swings to the right, now with **Afon Carrog** down to the left, until you reach a gate close to a stone bridge.

4. Continue onto the bridge, go through another gate, and follow the path along the grassy embankment above the river.

When the river bends away to the left, continue ahead for a few steps before veering slightly right, aiming for a **house and barn**. Cross a footbridge over a stream, bear left past the barn and then right around the side of the house. Cross the field ahead on a rough track that is marshy in places. Aim for a footpath sign and gate in the right-hand corner of the field.

5. Turn right along the road, cross a small bridge and continue past cottages and a drive on the left. Turn right at an old public footpath sign, follow the track to the **farm** and continue through the farmyard.

Continue through several gates onto a grassy track. Beyond another gate, veer right and cross a footbridge over a stream. Turn right and continue along the grassy path.

6. The track passes a cottage on the right and then a caravan park. Follow the road to the end and then turn left to reach the seafront car park at **Dinas Dinlle** to complete the walk. ♦

Prehistoric hilltop enclosure

Now eroded by the sea, Dinas Dinlle is an Iron Age hillfort crowning a glacial hillock, or drumlin. When the fort was built around 2,500 years ago it was surrounded by saltmarshes and had double, stone-walled ramparts and a heavily defended entrance. Finds of Roman pottery and coins support the idea that a mound on the summit may have been the site of a later Roman lighthouse.

On the coast path into Nant Gwrtheryn

Nant Gwrtheryn

Steep walking to an isolated valley and historic settlement in a stunning location

What to expect:
Field paths followed by steep walking on good paths. Steep road walking

Distance/time: 5km / 3¼ miles. Allow 2½-3 hours

Start: Free car park in the picnic area below Yr Eifl on the lane from Llithfaen signed to Nant Gwrtheryn.

Grid ref: SH 353 441

Ordnance Survey Map: Explorer 253 *Lleyn Peninsula West: Pwllheli, Abersoch & Aberdaron*

After the walk: Meinir Café (licensed) on the route in Nant Gwrtheryn. After the walk, pub in Llithfaen, pubs and shops in Nefyn

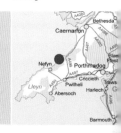

Walk outline

A walk through farmland with wide views of Llŷn's north coast is followed by a descent into the secluded valley of Nant Gwrtheryn. The excellent Meinir Café makes a great mid walk break where you can take in the stunning location over a snack and drink. The road is the only way out of the valley and this is followed steeply back to the car park.

Nant Gwrtheryn

Nant Gwrtheryn is one of Wales' most remarkable valleys. Hemmed in by sheer slopes on three sides, the remote quarrying settlement sits on a terrace facing out to sea. Abandoned for many years, the old buildings have now become a Welsh Language Centre with a conference centre and welcoming café for visitors.

Nant Gwrtheryn farm

The valley is named after Vortigern, the enigmatic British leader accused of foolishly betraying Britain to the Saxons in the fifth century. In an attempt to protect northern Britain from the Picts, he enlisted the help of Saxon mercenaries who then rebelled and set up their own kingdoms. Vortigern was blamed and pursued, and fled to this remote valley where he hid for the rest of his life.

Yellow horned poppy

The Walk

1. Turn right out of the car park and in about 100 metres bear right onto a **signed bridleway**. After a short walk across open ground pass under power lines and enter fields by a large gate. Go ahead, keeping to the right-hand field edge and passing a line of large boulders.

Go through the next gate and continue ahead until you reach a small gate in the wall on the right. Go through the gate and continue through the centre of the following field (with **two farms** below to the left) to pass through a small gap in the remains of an earth-covered stone wall.

Drop to a gate in the lower corner of the field. Go through the gate and follow a low earth bank ahead until you can turn right through a small gate in the wall. Turn left beside the wall to the corner, then turn right (ignore the stile or gate ahead) and follow the wall down to a **farm track** and turn right.

2. Immediately, the track forks—keep right, following the track which zig-zags down to **Ciliau Isaf**, a small hill farm overlooking the sea.

Go through a gate beside the farm buildings to reach a small gate below power lines. Go through the gate and bear half-right onto a descending footpath (part of the **Wales Coast Path**). This heads diagonally down the hillside through stunted oak woods clinging to the steeper ground on **Gallt y Bwlch**. Take care not to miss this; if a higher path is taken you will not be able to get down to the beach.

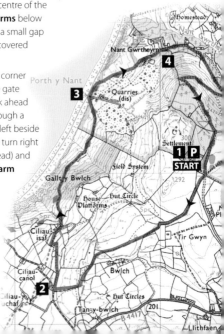

Nant Gwrtheryn: *A bird's-eye view of Nant Gwrtheryn*

3. Continue down to the shingle beach beside the old mining buildings and rusting machinery at **Porth y Nant**.

Beyond the ruins a good footpath rises past to the **Meinir Café** (a good place for a break) to join the road near the **Heritage Centre**.

4. Follow the road ahead, which becomes very steep higher up with superb views, back to the car park at point **1** to complete the walk. ♦

Vortigern's valley

Legend claims that Nant Gwytheryn, or 'Vortigern's Valley', was the last refuge of the disgraced British chieftain Vortigern. Today, the secluded valley and its redundant Victorian quarry houses, offices and chapel have been turned into a Welsh Language Centre. Complete with conference centre, restaurant and bar, and a rich programme of events, the centre now attracts more than 30,000 visitors a year.

Porth Dinllaen and Yr Eifl

@ Nefyn golf club

Porth Dinllaen

Easy walking to a unique historic sea port with a pub on the beach

What to expect:
Easy walking on access roads and well-used coastal path

Distance/time: 6.5km / 4 miles. Allow 3 hours

Start: Large National Trust car park at the end of 'Lon Golf' (Golf Lane) in Morfa Nefyn

Grid ref: SH 282 407

Ordnance Survey Map: Explorer 253 *Lleyn Peninsula West: Pwllheli, Abersoch & Aberdaron*

After the walk: On the walk there is the excellent 'Tŷ Coch Inn' at Porth Dinllaen (www.tycoch.co.uk).

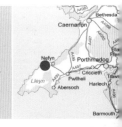

Walk outline

Easy walking on access roads leads across the golf course and down to the shore at Porth Dinllaen where you will find the lovely Tŷ Coch pub on the beach. From Porth Dinllaen the coastal path leads around the headland of Trwyn Porth Dinllaen and along the coast to the little cove of Aber Geirch. The route heads inland from here through fields and back across the golf course to Morfa Nefyn.

Trwyn Porth Dinllaen

Porth Dinllaen

Porth Dinllaen is one of the loveliest seaside settlements in North Wales and a popular location for pleasure boating and family holidays. Yet its idyllic setting today gives few clues to its previous importance as a major harbour and shipbuilding area, or the fact that it narrowly missed becoming the main ferry port for Ireland, instead of Holyhead, at the beginning of the nineteenth century.

The unique Tŷ Coch Inn, at Porth Dinllaen, perches on the edge of the beach and is often busy during the summer. Where else can you enjoy a pint on the beach? Opening times vary through the year, so check their website.

Thrift or 'sea pinks'

The Walk

1. Turn right out of the car park and follow the road to the **golf club** and '**RNLI House**'. Go through the gate onto the golf course and follow the rough, surfaced track across the golf course and down to **Porth Dinllaen**.

It is hard to believe, as you walk through this tiny hamlet, that in the eighteenth and early nineteenth centuries it was set to become one of the busiest sea ports in North Wales and for a time even rivalled Holyhead as the ferry port for Ireland. During this period

it had a shipyard and hotels to cater for travellers and plans were made for rapid expansion.

Arrangements were being made elsewhere to improve the road from Montgomeryshire to Porthmadog, where William Alexander Maddocks was shortly to build his great embankment across Traeth Mawr. With the new road in place and a recently formed Harbour

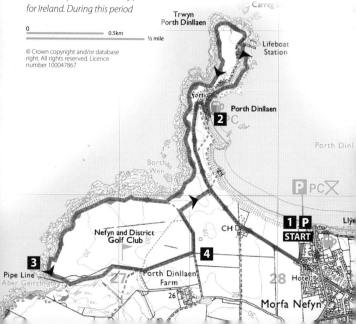

0   0.5km

½ mile

Frozen in time: *The sheltered hamlet of Port Dinllaen is an idyllic spot on the beach*

Company, Porth Dinllaen braced itself for great things. Prospects looked even more hopeful when a Parliamentary Bill was introduced to make Porth Dinllaen the packet port for Ireland replacing Holyhead. As things turned out, Holyhead won the day by just one vote!

It was a close call for Porth Dinllaen—this lovely spot has been largely undisturbed since the nineteenth century. The only boats you will see here today are small pleasure craft. And what a location!

Safe, sheltered waters with an unrivalled backdrop of shapely peaks falling sheer to the sea. The robust, stone-built cottages provide holiday accommodation, and where else can you get a pint on the beach?

2. Beyond the **Tŷ Coch Inn** a narrow, footpath passes between cottages at the base of the cliffs before continuing around several rocky coves just above the high water mark.

At the **Lifeboat Station** bear left up the concrete access road and where this swings sharp left at the top of the rise,

Sheltered waters: *Porth Dinllaen is one of the few bays on this coast to face east offering quiet, sheltered waters in a superb location*

bear right onto a higher, grassy path. Continue around the coast which is now more exposed and rugged, before rising to the coastguards' white-painted **lookout tower**.

The lookout is well placed with commanding views of Caernarfon Bay: from Holyhead Mountain on Anglesey all the way to the southwestern tip of Llŷn.

Pass below the lookout tower, then keep along the very edge of the **golf course**. Continue for 1½ miles / 3 kilometres.

3. At **Aber Geirch**—a small bay with a pipeline running into the water—turn inland and cross a stile out of the golf course. Follow the path into, then along a little valley beside the stream on the right ignoring a small footbridge (the continuation of the coastal path).

The stream soon bends right but the path continues ahead. Where the path bears to the right, go through a kissing gate ahead into fields. Bear left and walk beside the fence with **Porth Dinllaen Farm** away to the right and the golf course on the left.

4. At the next stile drop into a narrow

path enclosed by high earth banks. Turn left through a kissing gate and follow the path until it opens out onto the **golf course**. At the end of the bank on your left, turn sharp right and cross the golf course aiming for a large shed beside the road used earlier in the walk to reach Porth Dinllaen. Turn right along the road and retrace the outward journey to complete the walk. ◆

Pub on the beach!

The Tŷ Coch Inn at Porth Dinllaen started life as the vicarage for the local church at Edern. Built in 1823 of red bricks brought in as ballast from Holland, it was soon referred to locally as the Red House. But when a new vicarage was built beside the church, the house became one of four pubs on the beach serving the busy local shipbuilding industry.

Looking southwest from the slopes of Mynydd Anelog to Mynydd Mawr

Whistling Sands

A beautiful walk along the rugged coast from Whistling Sands to Mynydd Anelog

What to expect:
Good coastal path, narrow in places. Farmland paths sometimes with cattle

Distance/time: 6.75km / 4¼ miles. Allow 3-4 hours

Start: Large beach car park (National Trust) at Porth Oer (Whistling Sands) Fee payable

Grid ref: SH 166 295

Ordnance Survey Map: Explorer 253 *Lleyn Peninsula West: Pwllheli, Abersoch & Aberdaron*

After the walk: Beach Café at Porth Oer (Whistling Sands), pubs and cafés at Aberdaron, 4km / 2½ miles

Walk outline

From Whistling Sands a good coast path takes you along a lovely section of the rugged north coast—a mix of sea cliffs and small rocky coves. The coastal hill of Mynydd Anelog provides the focus of this route and after a short climb you will be able to enjoy the extensive view from its open exposed grassy summit. A return is made through flat farmland where there are sometimes cattle (lane option).

Whistling Sands

Whistling Sands, or Porth Oer, is the last of the sandy beaches on this exposed northern coast of Llŷn. From here on, high sea cliffs dominate all the way to Aberdaron. Shaped by the onshore winds and acidic soils, maritime heathlands bright with western gorse and heather dot the headland summits. This beautiful but scarce habitat is home to Llŷn's iconic choughs: acrobatic, crow-like birds with red legs and beaks.

Fresh local crab

Gulls, guillemots and razorbills nest on the cliffs, while gannets can often be seen passing, out to sea, or diving head first for shoals of fish. Keep your eyes peeled, too, for grey seals bobbing just offshore.

Gannet

The Walk

1. Walk down to the bottom of the car park and take the signed coastal path by the toilets. Go through the kissing gate above the beach and follow the coastal path for about 1 mile / 1.5 kilometres, passing the two islets of **Dinas Bach** and **Dinas Fawr**.

2. Just beyond Dinas Fawr there is an inlet and a small but distinct valley running inland—this is **Porthorion**. The path veers left-wards here and a link path leads inland to the road, but our way turns right at a marker post down into the valley to cross the stream by a small **wooden footbridge**. Rise directly up the slope from the footbridge to the corner of a field on the left. Walk ahead with the field to your left and in the far corner go through a gap and keep ahead on the rising path. This path makes its way directly through an area of rough open grazing land with a small farm away to the left. Continue straight ahead on a prominent, gently rising footpath, until you reach a grassy track in about 350 metres with a small cottage just over the rise to the left.

3. Bear right and follow the track as it curves up the hill. Keep right where the track forks and ignore a track on the left soon after. *At the top of the rise, there is a glorious view ahead along the cliffs to Mynydd Mawr, with Bardsey peeping over its shoulder.* Nearer at hand you will see a small cottage with a wall-enclosed field immediately in front on the slopes of Mynydd Anelog. Follow the track to the cottage.

4. Keep to the right of the cottage, then, at the end of the wall, bear half-left onto a rising

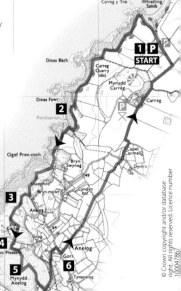

Final sandy bay: *Porth Oer is the last sandy bay on the north coast of Llŷn*

diagonal footpath which traverses the slopes of **Mynydd Anelog**. Pass above the cottage and continue until the two islands at Aberdaron come into view. To reach the summit take one of the narrow paths which rise to the right.

The summit is an excellent viewpoint with wide panoramas to the south and southwest across the wall-enclosed fields of Uwchmynydd—the 'Land's End of Llŷn', and the island of Bardsey (Ynys Enlli),

isolated by the chaotic tides of Bardsey Sound. East lie the wide bays at Aberdaron and Hell's Mouth, while northeast the view takes in the rocky coastline back to Whistling Sands and the headland of Penrhyn Mawr near Porth Iago. The pointed tops of Yr Eifl and Carn Fadryn can be seen in the distance.

This western extremity of Llŷn is characterised by an almost complete absence of trees—only the occasional hardy stump, often leaning dramatically inland, can stand against the harsh winter gales which blow in from the Irish Sea.

A treeless land: *The green treeless plateau of Uwchmynydd. The fields here are separated by low stone walls rather than hedgerows*

5. From the summit take the narrow footpath which heads in the direction of the two islands at Aberdaron. Lower down rejoin the traversing path above a **small cottage** surrounded by iron sculptures and turn right. About 100-150 metres after the cottage turn sharp left onto a footpath which passes through an unusual gate (immediately before power lines) into a small field. Go ahead to pass through another decorative gate and beside a second cottage on the right. Follow the obvious footpath ahead (ignore minor paths on either side) down towards cottages. Go through a gate and follow a path beside a cottage to join the access track. Follow this track to the road.

6. Go right along the road and after about 100 metres, turn left onto a farm track which leads past **Gors farmhouse** and into fields by farm outbuildings. The right of way now takes a direct line through a number of fields and is well supplied with stiles which mark the route. Sometimes you follow the field edge, sometimes you cut through the centre of the field.

There are often cattle in these fields, if

you find this a problem turn left at point **6** and follow the lane instead.

In the last field as you approach outbuildings and houses, cross a stile immediately before the outbuildings and turn left up the field to enter a lane by a stile. Turn left, then immediately right, signed to 'Whistling Sands'.

The lane can now be followed back to the car park at **Porth Oer**. ♦

Graded grains

Whistling Sands gets its name form the curious whistling or squeaking sound made by the sand when walked on. This is caused by the unusual shape of the sand particles and is achieved by lightly striking the sand with the sole of your foot as you bring it forward with each step. It only seems to work on the hard, partly dried out sand.

Bardsey (Ynys Enlli) from Mynydd Mawr

Aberdaron

A spectacular walk over two coastal hills with some stunning views over the treeless landscape of Uwchmynydd

What to expect:
Good coastal path and field paths. Some stretches along quiet lanes

Distance/time: 9.5km / 6 miles. Allow 2-3 hours

Start: Parking is limited to a large National Trust pay and display car park in the centre of Aberdaron. Alternative parking at point **3**, below Mynydd Mawr (SH 143 255)

Grid ref: SH 172 264

Ordnance Survey Map: Explorer 253 *Lleyn Peninsula West: Pwllheli, Abersoch & Aberdaron*

After the walk: Pubs and cafés in Aberdaron

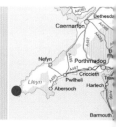

Walk outline

From Aberdaron, the route follows the coast path to a tiny cove, then swings inland via lanes and field paths to reach the western tip of Llŷn opposite the enigmatic isle of Bardsey. Excellent walking along a fine stretch of the new Wales Coast Path with superb views out to Bardsey completes the round with a return to Aberdaron.

Aberdaron

Aberdaron is the only settlement of any size in this remote corner of Wales. Despite its compact nature it has been firmly on the map since the Middle Ages as the penultimate destination on what, in its day, would have been an arduous journey: the Pilgrimage to Bardsey, or Ynys Enlli. Bands of pilgrims gathered at Aberdaron to wait for favourable weather for the final leg of their journey over the tidal sound to Ynys Enlli, or Bardsey—'island of 20,000 saints'.

Today, the rugged coastline around Aberdaron promises some of the finest coastal walking in Wales. The elevated cliff paths are perfect, too, for spotting Atlantic grey seals, porpoise and common or bottlenose dolphins.

Overlooking Bardsey

Curious grey seal

End of the line: *Aberdaron was the end of the 'Saint's Road'*

The Walk

1. Turn right out of the car park, cross the **old bridge** and pass between buildings ahead to reach the beach. Turn right along the sand.

Aberdaron was traditionally the end of the 'Saint's Road' taken by pilgrims en-route to Bardsey during the Middle Ages. An indication of the difficulty of the journey in those days is given by the fact that three pilgrimages to Bardsey were said to equal one to Rome.

Aberdaron is also the birth place of Richard Robert Jones or 'Dic Aberdaron', who was born on a nearby farm in 1780. Although his parents were probably illiterate, he reputedly learned to speak fluently and write in more than 14 languages. His love of foreign tongues and books took him on travels all over the country and his bizarre appearance, peculiar dress and unusual talent has turned him into a folklore figure. He died in 1843 at the age of 63 and is buried at St Asaph church.

Ford the shallow river and continue to the far end of the bay. Go through the kissing gate and climb steps up to the cliff top coastal path. Turn left and follow the path to **Porth Meudwy**, also known as 'Fisherman's Cove', where steps lead down into the little cove.

2. Turn inland (right) from here following a track up the little valley between high bracken-covered banks. Just before the track swings right, bear left on a narrow footpath to cross a footbridge and rise steeply to a small **farm and campsite**. Go ahead through the site to a lane. Turn right along the lane and after about 100 metres take the signed footpath on the left between fields. At a second lane turn right, then, in about 20 metres turn left down the access track to a stone cottage, **Pen y Maes**.

Bear left through a kissing gate just before the cottage garden and follow an enclosed footpath to cross a stile adjacent to the cottage. Cut directly across the next two fields aiming for an **old farmhouse**. Go through a gate beside the farm and follow a track down to the lane. Turn left along the lane.

3. After a cattle grid, the lane enters the **National Trust land** at **Braich-y-Pwll**. Here, immediately before the lane swings right up onto **Mynydd Mawr**, bear left off the road on a footpath beside the wall/fence. Turn left at the corner of the wall and a little further on

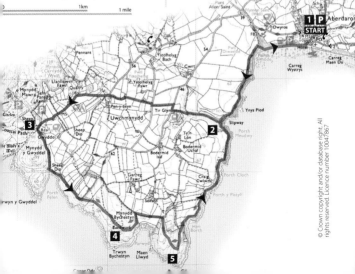

Pilgrim's goal: *Bardsey was the spiritual goal of pilgims throughout the Middle Ages*

go through the a gate on the left. Follow the path ahead along the cliff edge to go through a second gate. The path continues ahead through a more open area beside fenced fields on the left. Go through another gate in the wall and keep ahead again.

4. Continue until you reach a point almost level with a small rocky islet, known as **Carreg Ddu**, out to the right. The path swings left now up over steeper ground with the deep cliff-lined inlet of **Parwyd** to the right. At the top

of the rise you meet a fence with a large white boulder on the far side. Turn left along the fence to a kissing gate by a National Trust stone pillar (**Bychestyn**) in the upper field corner. Turn right through the kissing gate and follow the field edge ahead to a gate in the far corner. Go through the gate and walk ahead again to a gate on the right that leads onto the headland of **Pen y Cil**.

5. Follow the path ahead past the cairn and continue down beside the fence on the left. Lower down the path swings left, passes through a kissing gate and continues ahead with a small walled field on the right. Beyond a second

kissing gate the path keeps to the outer edge of fields on the left on the very edge of the steep coastal slope. Continue to **Porth Meudwy**—a tiny inlet where the path descends steps.

Porth Meudwy is the embarkation point for boat trips to Bardsey

From Porth Meudwy climb the steps ahead and follow the coastal path back to **Aberdaron**. ♦

Ancient fields

The rocky, treeless headland of Uwchmynydd has been farmed continuously since Neolithic times. Late prehistoric and early medieval hut circles and house platforms survive on the south flank of Mynydd Mawr, while the names of local farms such as Llawenan, Meillionydd and Ysgo date from the Middle Ages. Continued low-intensity farming means many of the medieval and post-medieval fields and drystone walls can still be seen today.

The broad sweep of Hell's Mouth from the slopes of Mynydd Rhiw

Rhiw & Porth Ysgo

An easy walk over the headland of Penarfynydd with dramatic views to Bardsey and Hell's Mouth

What to expect:
Good coastal paths through open heather with wide views

Distance/time: 8km / 5 miles. Allow 3-4 hours

Start: Begin the walk in the little village of Rhiw. From the crossroads in the middle of the village go south along a narrow lane for about 400 metres to where the lane forks.

Grid ref: SH 224 274

Ordnance Survey Map: Explorer 253 *Lleyn Peninsula West: Pwllheli, Abersoch & Aberdaron*

After the walk: Pubs, and cafés in Aberdaron

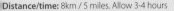

Walk outline

Starting in the hamlet of Rhiw farm lanes are followed to reach a picturesque and isolated cove at Porth Ysgo. The coast path is then followed over the headland of Penarfynydd with its wide views along the coast to Bardsey and across the gulf of Hell's Mouth.

Mynydd Rhiw

Rhiw is a small, rocky parish on the slopes above Hell's Mouth. Characterised by scattered cottages surrounded by small walled fields, the area has been settled since prehistoric times. Neolithic stone axes and flint blades have often been found across the parish, and a stone axe factory was excavated on Mynydd Rhiw in 1956. There are Neolithic burial chambers, or cromlechs, at Tan y Muriau and Tyn Fron, with later standing stones, hut circles and an Iron Age hillfort nearby.

On the western slopes above Hell's Mouth is Plas yn Rhiw, a small, atmospheric 16th-century manor house surrounded by intimate gardens. Now owned by the National Trust, it's well worth a visit.

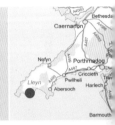

Abandoned tractor

Peregrine

Patchwork of fields: *The slopes of Mynydd Rhiw from Penarfynydd*

The Walk

1. Ignoring the left fork, walk down the lane with fine views west towards Mynydd Mawr, Mynydd Anelog, Aberdaron and Bardsey.

At the gateway to **Penarfynydd**, a stone-built farmhouse at the end of the lane, you have a choice. Either bear left through the farmyard and continue from point **2**, or, for a detour to the secluded cove of Porth Ysgo, go through the large gate ahead, turn right immediately through a second large gate and walk through the fields beside the fence on your right to enter a quiet lane by a stile. Turn left along the lane and about 75 metres beyond a sharp right-hand bend, a signed footpath with two kissing gates on the left leads down the small valley of **Nant y Gadwen**.

At the lower end of the valley, bear right through a kissing gate onto National Trust land. This brings you to the top of the cliffs above **Porth Ysgo** and a fine view along the coast to Porth Cadlan and the rocky isle of Maen Gwenonwy.

Follow the path down a flight of steps to reach the sandy beach.

Retrace your steps to Penarfynydd.

2. At the farm bear right (or left if you did not visit Porth Ysgo) through the farmyard to a gate to the left of the farmhouse. Go through the gate and bear right onto a path beside the wall. This soon bears left away from the wall onto the headland at **Mynydd Penarfynydd** above Trwyn Talfarach.

In clear conditions this exposed headland offers spectacular views of the coast both to the east and west. Westwards, steep cliffs line the coast to Trwyn y Penrhyn, with the two islands of Ynys Gwylan Fawr and Ynys Gwylan Bach ('large gull island' and 'little gull island') and Bardsey beyond. Eastwards the view takes in the wide sweep of Porth Neigwl or Hell's Mouth, enclosed to the south by the green peninsula of Mynydd Cilan. The mountains of Snowdonia line the far horizon and lead the eye south along Cardigan Bay to Saint David's Head if you are lucky.

3. Double back now but don't follow the path back to Penarfynydd, instead, take one of the paths which soon fork right to follow the crest of the broad flat ridge to the **triangulation pillar** on the highest point at 177 metres.

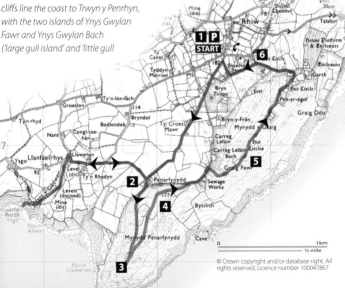

Land's End of North Wales: *A panorama looking west from Rhiw towards Aberdaron and Bardsey*

4. Continue northwards along the ridge descending gently. Go through a gate and continue to the field corner where a stile leads over the wall and onto a track by a small sewage works. Follow the rising track towards cottages ahead. Before you reach the cottages look for a stile over the wall on the right by a gate. Cross the stile and walk ahead past a large rock outcrop on the left. Soon the path curves left-wards to contour the grassy hillside above the vast expanse of **Hell's Mouth**.

5. Continue ahead rising gently and ignoring footpaths on the right and left. Eventually the footpath runs beside old stone walls on the right enclosing ancient fields. A little further on pass a small **stone cottage built from huge rocks** in a spectacular position overlooking the bay. The path forks here—bear left up away from the wall and overhead power lines. The path crosses the crest of the rocky ridge and continues ahead to join a broad path coming up from the right. Bear left along the path past a cottage on the left. Immediately before the next cottage, turn left and follow a path

beside the wall to stone steps in the corner of the field.

6. Over the steps turn right past a house on the right. Continue over the open field beyond the house to reach the access track to a cottage over to the left. Turn right along the track and go through the gate into the lane. Turn left for a few metres to complete the walk. ♦

Ship's graveyard

Porth Neigwl, better known as 'Hell's Mouth', was notorious for shipwrecks in the age of sail. Enclosed by the two rocky headlands of Mynydd Cilan and Mynydd Penarfynydd, the bay's wide mouth and southwest orientation made it the perfect trap for sailing ships. Caught by the prevailing winds, ships were blown into the bay, quickly passing the point of no return and were doomed.

Heather and gorse on Mynydd Cilan common

Mynydd Cilan

A circuit of a dramatic headland with superb views in all directions in clear weather

What to expect:
Good coastal path for much of the time. Some farmland paths and occasional lanes too

Distance/time: 11km / 6½ miles. Allow 3-4 hours

Start: Free parking in a small beach car park at the southeastern end of Hell's Mouth near the village of Llanengan

Grid ref: SH 248 266

Ordnance Survey Map: Explorer 253 *Lleyn Peninsula West: Pwllheli, Abersoch & Aberdaron*

After the walk: Sun Inn, Llanengan. Pubs and cafés in Abersoch

Walk outline

Beginning on the storm beach at Hell's Mouth, the route follows the Wales Coast Path up onto the headland of Mynydd Cilan. Easy walking over open heather around Mynydd Cilan to Porth Ceiriad with a return through fields and farmland to complete the walk.

Mynydd Cilan headland

Mynydd Cilan is part of a spectacular 10-kilometre stretch of heath-covered sea cliff between Hell's Mouth and Abersosch now designated a Special Protection Area. This important and beautiful coastal habitat is a rich mix of coastal and maritime heathland, maritime grassland and 'unimproved' pastures that is ablaze with colour in summer. The heath is dominated by heather and gorse and dotted with small pools that support lizards and other reptiles, and unusual plants such pillwort, three-lobed water-crowsfoot and chamomile.

Pony trekking

The high sea cliffs provide breeding sites for guillemots, razorbills, kittiwakes and fulmars. The short, cliff-top turf is also ideal habitat for choughs whose acrobatic flight and high 'chow, chow' calls help define this lovely coast.

Stonechat

The Walk

1. From the car park, follow the footpath down to the beach and turn left.

At the end of the beach, bear left up to a stile. Cross the stile and take the path that forks left almost immediately. The path heads diagonally-left up through the bracken to pass above a farm down to the left. Ignore a footpath on the right at the top of the rise, instead,

continue ahead to a stile into a sloping field. Cross the stile and go ahead (ignore the stile on the left) at first, then swing right up the bank between gorse bushes to the corner of the field where there are two gates and a house beyond. Go through the right-hand gate and bear left around the right-hand side of the house and its garden (**Greenland**) to join the access track. Turn right along the access track.

2. Go through a kissing gate at the end of the track onto the open common land of **Mynydd Cilan**. Bear right past cottages and chalets until you reach the corner of the wall/fence on the right (within 300 metres). Turn right here past a small reedy pool and follow a good grassy path ahead. Turn left and follow the good path across the common. At a path junction turn right and continue keeping to the right of small fields to reach an **Ordnance Survey triangulation pillar**.

In clear conditions there are wide views from here across Hell's Mouth to Mynydd Rhiw and distant Bardsey at the extreme western end of Llŷn. To the southeast there are distant views to the mountains of Snowdonia including Cadair Idris and the serrated skyline of the Rhinog hills.

Open pools: *Ponies graze alongside one of the many pools on Mynydd Cilan common*

Continue on the broad path beyond the triangulation pillar as it curves left around the headland. Stay on the open grass footpath following the Coast Path waymarkers until directed left almost at the southern tip of the headland on **Trwyn Cilan**.

3. The path now makes its way between gorse bushes and bracken until you reach fields enclosed by walls and fences ahead. Don't go through the gate ahead, instead turn right and walk down beside the wall and fence. Near the cliff edge, go through the kissing gate on the left and walk down beside the fence with the cliff edge close by on the right. *Take care:* the path between the fence and the cliff edge is not very wide here.

4. Lower down go through a small gate to enter a section of permissive footpath enclosed by fences. Follow this path to a footbridge over a stream.

Cross the footbridge and follow the path inland to go through a kissing gate and on up the rising path to another kissing gate to enter fields. Head directly

Wide skies: *Mynydd Cilan enjoys wide views over Hell's Mouth and inland to the hills of Llŷn and Snowdonia on the horizon*

through the field to go through a kissing gate in the far corner, then bear right along the field edge to another kissing gate and field gate in the corner. In the following field bear diagonally-right to the corner by a farm. Go through the kissing gate and head left along the access track to a lane. Turn right along the lane for about ½ mile / 1 kilometre, to the **Bethlehem Chapel** on the left.

5. Take the signed footpath on the left immediately after the chapel. Walk

beside the building, go through a kissing gate, then head across fields to an access road. Turn left, then right almost immediately, down the driveway to **a cottage**. Pass the front of the cottage and keep ahead passing old stone outbuildings to enter a small field. Walk ahead along the field edge through a small gate into a farm track.

6. Turn left along the track and as you approach **Bachwared farm** bear right onto a path to the right of the farmhouse. Go through a kissing gate and keep ahead to a gate into a sloping field. Walk down the field keeping to the left edge beside the fence.

ook for a gap in the fence on the left (coast path waymark) well before you each **Nant Farm** at the bottom of the field. Turn left here down into a small valley to cross a **footbridge** over the stream and a stile beyond. Go ahead to cross a stile on the right used earlier in the walk. Retrace the outward route back down to the beach and car park to complete the walk. ♦

Heathland, choughs and dolphins

In summer, Mynydd Cilan's heathland is bright with purple heather, yellow-flowered western gorse and emerald green bilberry. A beautiful blend of coastal and maritime heath and 'unimproved' pasture, dotted with small pools, and flanked by traditional field banks—or cloddiau, this rare habitat supports lizards, stonechats, wheatears and breeding choughs. It's also a great place for seawatching: with common and bottle-nosed dolphins frequently seen.

The picturesque harbour at Abersoch

Abersoch

A walk along a beautiful beach at Abersoch followed by a circuit of an impressive rocky headland

What to expect:

Easy walking along a sandy beach followed by good paths over open heather

Distance/time: 9km / 5¾ miles. Allow 3½ hours

Start: There is a small layby on the outskirts of Abersoch on the Llanbedrog road with free parking for a handful of cars. This is opposite the access to the beach at Trwyn y Fach

Grid ref: SH 315 290

Ordnance Survey Map: Explorer 253 *Lleyn Peninsula West: Pwllheli, Abersoch & Aberdaron*

After the walk: Pubs, tearooms, cafés and restaurants in Abersoch

Walk outline

Easy paths through the dunes at Trwyn y Fach are followed by a walk along the golden sands of Abersoch's famous beach. The walk then changes completely with a climb onto the rocky, open headland at Mynydd Tir-cwmwd with its wide views and spectacular setting. A circuit of the headland is made before a return along the beach.

Abersoch

Abersoch needs little introduction: famed for its exclusive holiday developments, water sports and surfing shops, this tiny village springs to life in the holiday season when its single street is full to bursting. For walkers, the town offers a good selection of food shops, pubs, restaurants, cafés and takeaways; outside the main holiday period, you will have them to yourself.

Fishing floats

Abersoch is named after its sheltered location at the mouth of the curious Afon Soch. This short river seems to flow backwards. Its strange route from the adjacent valley through a short gorge to enter the sea here rather than at Hell's Mouth is one of Lleyn's many topographical puzzles.

Herring gull

The Walk

1. Cross the road and walk down through the dunes of **Trwyn y Fach** to the beach and turn left along the sand.

2. At the end of the beach and immediately after the final chalet, turn left up a sandy track to join a tarmac road. Follow it as it rises gently.

3. In just under ½ mile / 1 kilometre and opposite the gate to **Garreg-fawr** take the signed coastal path on the right. This leads up onto the open ground of **Mynydd Tir-cwmwd**. The path climbs steeply, aided by stone steps here and there, up onto the open common.

At the top of the rise turn right and follow the path through the bracken. At a T-junction, turn right and follow the main path around the headland ignoring minor paths on the left.

4. Near the front of the headland the path drops a little and there are a number of variations, but coast path waymarkers keep you on the right path.

Continue to the **Tin Man** statue on the cliffs overlooking the beach at **Llanbedrog**.

At the top of the cliffs there is a grand view of Llanbedrog and the bay stretching east towards Pwllheli, while the hills of Garn Boduan, Carn Fadryn and Yr Eifl are backed by the higher summits of Snowdonia to the northeast.

5. Beyond the statue, the coast path descends the steep hillside by means of steps and handrails. Don't take this path, instead take the path on the left. This heads up through the trees and beside

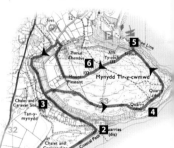

rocks to reach the open hill top. Follow the obvious path to the summit, marked by **benches and a large viewfinder**.

6. From the viewfinder walk to the **triangulation pillar** on the summit and take the path straight ahead (ignore paths to the left and right).

0   1km

½ mile

Bird's eye view: *There is a superb view of Llanbedrog from the cliffs beside the Tin Man*

Follow the path to a T-junction just before a cottage and turn right. In a few metres join the driveway to the cottage and follow this to reach a tarmac lane. Turn left down the lane passing houses and cottages on both sides.

At a T-junction turn left and follow the descending lane. Pass **Geufron** on the left and where the lane forks, bear left.

Follow the lane down to the car park near the beach. Turn right along the beach and retrace the outward route to complete the walk. ♦

Headland figure

High on the headland of Mynydd Tir-cwmwd, above Llanbedrog, is Llŷn's famous 'Tin Man'. The first sculpture on the headland was a wooden ship's figurehead erected in 1919 by the owner of nearby Plas Glyn y Weddw. It was later replaced by an iron figure by local sculptor, Simon van de Put. When that finally rusted away, the current 'Tin Man' was helicoptered in, in June 2002.

Criccieth Castle and seafront

Criccieth & Llanystumdwy

An easy walk from a historic seaside town, across a sandy beach to the birth place of a well known Prime Minister

What to expect:
Well marked coast path, farm tracks and country lanes

Distance/time: 7km / 4½ miles. Allow 2½ - 3 hours

Start: Small car park at West Parade (at the westerly end of Marine Terrace, west of the castle) in Criccieth

Grid ref: SH 495 376

Ordnance Survey Map: Explorer 254 *Lleyn Peninsula East: Porthmadog, Criccieth & Pwllheli*

After the walk: Cafés, pubs and restaurants in Criccieth town centre

Walk outline

The walk begins at the western edge of the town and continues west on the Wales Coast Path to reach a sandy beach at the mouth of the Afon Dwyfor. Here the route veers inland to follow the river before heading north through farmland to the village of Llanystumdwy. The return walk to Criccieth is made along a quiet country lane.

Criccieth

The brooding ruins of medieval Criccieth Castle dominate this pretty seaside town. High on its rock, Criccieth is the only one of Edward I's Welsh coastal fortresses that sits on an earlier native foundation. Much of the inner castle was built by Llywelwyn ap Iowerth, or 'Llywelwyn the Great', around 1230. He cruelly imprisoned his illegitimate eldest son, Gruffyd, in its dungeons to prevent him becoming his successor. Criccieth's name is thought to come from two Welsh words: *crug* and *caeth*, which translate literally as 'prisoner's rock'.

Lloyd-George museum

Today, this distinctive town is a popular destination for tourists, who come to enjoy the broad beaches, historic town and famous Cadwalader's ice cream.

Oystercatcher

The Walk

1. Face the sea and turn right to follow the tarmac path and soon reach a Wales Coast Path signpost. Walk on along the path above the beach, with a fence to the right and the sea down to the left.

Continue through a wooden gate and stay ahead as the path widens slightly. As you approach a **derelict cliff-edge cottage** follow the path as it veers to the right, then turn left at the waymarker to head back towards the sea.

2. The path soon drops down to the beach, near a National Trust sign. Continue along the beach; if the tide is high, take the path at the top of the beach.

Follow the high-tide line around the pebbly headland and as you turn the corner you'll see the mouth of **Afon Dwyfor** ahead below **Glan-y-mor**. Don't attempt to cross the river but bear right passing low sandy bluffs to a grassy path beside the river. Follow this, now with the river on your left.

Afon Dwyfor begins its watery journey 12 kilometres away in the valley of Cwm Pennant at the foothills of Moel Hebog. It flows south through the villages of Dolbenmaen and Llanystumdwy before spilling into Tremadog Bay here.

Eventually go through a kissing gate, along the boardwalk and continue to follow the river path. Veer slightly

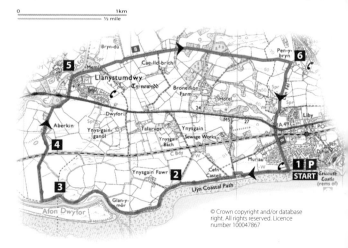

0   1km
½ mile

Castle on the beach: *Criccieth Castle seen from the pebbly beach below the coast path*

right just before a stone platform to go through a gate.

3. Follow the path along the field edge, keeping the fence on your left. Go through the metal kissing gate and turn right, following the waymarkers. Stay on this track now as it leads out of the field and towards the **railway line**. Cross the stile and then the single track railway line with care.

4. Cross another stile and follow the track towards **Aberkin** farmhouse. Go

through the first gate by the farm then almost immediately go over a stile by a second gate (if the gate is closed). Follow the concrete farm drive passing cottages and then the farm buildings. Eventually reach the main road and cross carefully to go through a small gate ahead; continue along the narrow lane between houses.

You have now reached the village of Llanystumdwy, which is famous for being the childhood home of David Lloyd George, Liberal Prime Minister of Britain from 1916 – 1922. There is a museum at

Criccieth panorama: *Seen from Castle hill, the view spans Criccieth seafront, Moel-y-Gest and the hills of Snowdonia beyond*

Highgate, the house where he lived as a boy (open Easter and May – September).

5. At the end of the road turn left, then immediately right before the bridge, at the signpost for **Lloyd George's grave** to pass a terrace of houses. The turning for the grave is on the left.

David Lloyd George died in 1945, aged 82, and was buried here by the river. The monument was designed by Clough Williams Ellis, architect and founder of Portmeirion village.

Leave the grave and turn left to continue along the lane. Follow this road for almost 1½ miles / 4 kilometres, passing **Tŷ Newydd** and then the fisheries.

Tŷ Newydd is the National Writers' Centre for Wales and since 1990 has been running courses for writers who visit from all over the world. There has been a house here since the 16th century, but the main part of the property as it stands today was built during the mid-18th century. It was later the home of David Lloyd George when his family moved in with his uncle, Richard Lloyd.

6. When you reach 30 mph road signs

with a housing estate ahead, turn right (signposted for the 'No. 8 cycle route'). Continue on this lane to the main road. Cross it and bear slightly left and then turn right down **Lôn Fêl** at the signpost for the beach and castle. Cross the railway, pass the scout hut and follow the road towards the sea to reach the car park to complete the walk. ♦

Criccieth Castle

Llywelyn the Great built the first castle on this site around 1230, but this consisted of little more than a fortified tower. The ruins visible today were built as part of Edward I's 'iron ring' of fortresses positioned all along the Welsh coast. They are fine examples of ground-breaking medieval castle architecture and became a symbol of Edward's determination to assert his authority over the Welsh.

Afon Glaslyn and Cnicht seen from Borth-y-Gest

Borth-y-Gest

A moderate walk from a picturesque village and along two superb beaches

Distance/time: 6.5km / 4 miles. Allow 2 hours

Start: Car park in Borth-y-Gest (at the southern end of the bay, opposite the café and shop)

Grid ref: SH 565 375

Ordnance Survey Map: Explorer 254 *Lleyn Peninsula East: Porthmadog, Criccieth & Pwllheli*

After the walk: Cafés and restaurants in Borth-y-Gest and Porthmadog

Walk outline

The walk starts at the village of Borth-y-Gest and follows the coast path westwards as it explores rocky coves and sandy beaches, before dropping onto Black Rock Sands; a long stretch of sand with great views extending south along Cardigan Bay and to the end of the Llŷn Peninsula on a clear day. The return journey is made across golf links and through a scenic caravan park.

Borth-y-Gest

Borth-y-Gest's tiny harbour hummed with activity during the nineteenth century. Boatbuilding yards lined the waterfront, turning out robust ships that set sail from Porthmadog harbour. Slate from the Ffestiniog hills was exported all over the world, and many of the graceful schooners and yachts that carried Wales' precious 'grey gold' were built here in Borth-y-Gest.

The Powder House

Before the Cob was built across the river mouth in the early 1800s, Borth-y-Gest was also the starting point for the dangerous short cut across the Glaslyn Estuary. Experienced villagers risked their lives to guide travellers across the treacherous tidal sands to Harlech on the far side.

Common tern

The Walk

1. Face away from the **harbour** and walk up a short path at the top left corner of car park; turn left at the top.

The line of four tall houses here on the left are called the Pilot Houses—they once housed pilots that looked out for incoming ships and escorted them through the shallow estuary waters. Most of the terraces here once housed maritime families—the size of the house dependent on rank.

As the road sweeps right, stay ahead and as the road ends keep ahead again following the footpath; pass a **small church** above on the right.

Look behind you here for great views over the Cob and the Moelwyn and Cnicht mountains behind.

Continue ahead on the clear path with sandy coves below on the left; ignore steps on the left.

2. Eventually, at a T-junction of slatted paths shortly after upward steps, ignore the right fork and stay ahead. Cross the footbridge and go down to the **beach**. Aim for the large sand dune straight ahead and as you reach it look towards the bottom right-hand corner for a path uphill bearing right to become a clear path that snakes upwards and levels out.

Turn left at the top and walk beside the stone wall. The path ends at a footpath sign and a rough drive. Turn right through the (usually) open gate then immediately left. Follow the path to reach steep steps and follow them

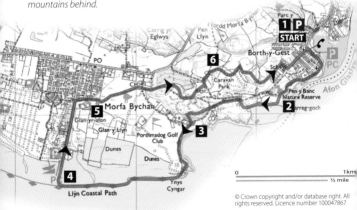

River mouth: *Ynys Cyngar and the Powder House near the mouth of Afon Glaslyn*

as they zig-zag downhill to reach a concrete slipway.

3. Either turn left down the slipway then right onto beach; or if tide is high go straight over and follow a stony path on top of the embankment with the golf course on the right.

Aim for **Ynys Cyngar**, the rocky outcrop ahead with a small house just visible.

This tiny white cottage is known as 'Powder House' because gunpowder for the

slate mines of Ffestiniog was off-loaded from passing boats and stored here.

If the tide is out then skirt around the edge of the rocks and to the left of the house. If not, continue along the embankment path to the right of the house and pass above it before dropping down to **Black Rock Sands**.

Once on the beach, continue ahead with dunes to the right, for almost ½ mile / 1 kilometre. Cross a stream (which may be deep at high tide or after heavy rain).

Black Rock Sands gets its name from the

Inland waters: *Borth-y-Gest occupies a beautiful location at the mouth of the Glaslyn estuary*

dark cliffs that line its western end. It's a popular film location—it featured in a music video by British band Supergrass and in a film version of Macbeth. It was also the backdrop for the Manic Street Preachers album cover This is my truth tell me yours.

4. Take the first main exit you reach on the right (look for a sign-board and blue cabin) passing toilets then caravan parks. Soon after the **Glanaber** pub take a right turn for **Y Ffridd**, then soon follow a public footpath sign on the right leading into a wooded area to emerge onto a **golf course**.

5. Turn left to follow the wide gravel path across the course. After a large bend and fence posts, the track meets a tarmac road. Turn left, then almost immediately right to walk along a fence to a path uphill into trees. Continue until you emerge at a caravan park, then turn left.

At a junction after the **tennis courts**, go slightly left then immediately right (with a duck pond to your right and a cabin on the left). Follow this winding road uphill, eventually passing two wooden refuse bin stores.

5. At the first caravan on your left and a slate sign for 'Borth-y-Gest and Beach' ahead, turn right to cross a small grassy clearing, leading to a path through trees, then fork left and go through the gate.

Follow the path downhill, behind school buildings then through a kissing gate. Turn right to pass the back of houses, then left at road, down **Mersey Street** to complete the walk. ♦

Parc-y-Borth

Parc-y-Borth is a large, 25 acre local nature reserve in Borth-y-Gest, accessible by a footpath near the garage. Perched on a hillside above the village, its ancient oak woodland and two small wildflower meadows are a haven for wildlife. Look out for greater spotted woodpeckers, tawny owls and pied flycatchers in early summer. From the summit, there are broad views over the Glaslyn Estuary, too..

Useful Information

Wales Coast Path

Comprehensive information about all sections of the **Wales Coast Path** can be found at: www.walescoastpath.co.uk and www.walescoastpath.gov.uk

Visit Wales

The Visit Wales website covers everything from accommodation and events to attractions and adventure. For information on the area covered by this book, see: www.visitwales.co.uk

Tourist Information Centres

The main TICs provide free information on everything from accommodation and travel to what's on and walking advice

Caernarfon	01286 672232	caernarfon.tic@gwynedd.gov.uk
Abersoch	01758 712929	enquiries@abersochandllyn.co.uk
Pwllheli	01758 613000	pwllheli.tic@gwynedd.gov.uk
Porthmadog	01766 512981	porthmadog.tic@gwynedd.gov.uk

Travel

Public Transport for services in all parts of Wales are available from Traveline Cymru. Call 0871 200 22 33 or see: **www.traveline-cymru.info**

For details of steam railways in North Wales, along with timetables and prices, see **www.greatlittletrainsofwales.co.uk**

Tide Times

Some walks depend on tide times, and it's important to check before starting out. For details see **www.tourism.ceredigion.gov.uk/saesneg/tides.htm** and calculate the tide times according to location. You can also pick up traditional Tide Tables from TICs for around £1

Weather

The Met Office operates a 24 hour online weather forecast

Follow the link from the National Park website **www.eryri-npa.gov.uk/visiting/your-weather-forecast-service** or see www.metoffice.gov.uk